REAL ESTATE EXAM PREP

CONNECTICUT

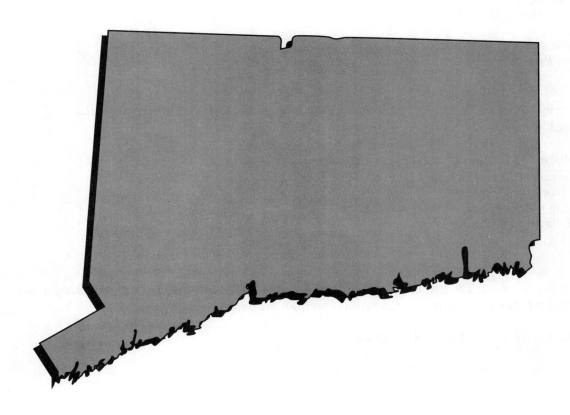

Dearborn™

Real Estate Education

While a great deal of care has been taken to provide accurate and current information, the ideas, suggestions, general principles, and conclusions presented in this text are subject to local, state and federal laws and regulations, court cases, and any revisions of same. The reader is urged to consult legal counsel regarding any points of law. This publication should not be used as a substitute for competent legal advice.

Publisher: Evan M. Butterfield
Senior Development Editor: Kristen Short
Development Editor: Amanda Rahn
Associate Development Editor: Michael J. Scafuri
Senior Managing Editor: Ronald J. Liszkowski
Art Manager: Lucy Jenkins
Cover Design: Gail Chandler

Testbank Reviewer: Katherine A. Pancak
Exam Prep Series Content Consultant: Marie Spodek, DREI

Published by Dearborn™ Real Estate Education,
a division of Dearborn Financial Publishing, Inc.®
155 North Wacker Drive
Chicago, IL 60606-1719
http://www.dearbornRE.com

Introduction

Welcome to *Connecticut Exam Prep*! When you bought this book, you showed that you are serious about passing the exam and getting your real estate license. This is *NOT* an easy test. For people whose test-taking skills are weak, or who haven't adequately prepared, the exam can be a nightmare. For those who have taken the time and effort to study and review, however, the exam can be a much more positive experience.

It's pretty obvious, though, that if you practice and review key material, your test score will improve. This book is your key to exam success.

The process is simple: Just work your way through the practice questions, taking your time and answering each one carefully. Then check your answers by studying the Answer Key, where you'll find both the correct answer to each question as well as an explanation of *why* that answer is correct. It might be a good idea to review your classroom materials and textbook before you start.

Remember: These 202 questions reflect as closely as possible the topic coverage of the state-specific portion of your exam only! For the balance of the test, you'll need to use a "national" exam prep book. And remember, too, that it takes study and hard work on your part to pass the licensing exam: no single study aid will do the trick alone.

Experts who are familiar with the Connecticut licensing examination, as well as real estate law and practice, prepared this book. You've taken the first step toward your success as a real estate professional: Good Luck!

Dearborn Real Estate Education

1. Mark, a licensed broker, procures a ready, willing, and able buyer for his seller principal. The seller accepts the buyer's offer in writing, then experiences a change of heart and withdraws the acceptance. In this situation, Mark

   1. is entitled to collect a commission.
   2. is without recourse because the transaction was never completed.
   3. may sue the buyer.
   4. may retain the deposit as commission.

2. A real estate company has entered into agency agreements with both a seller and a buyer. The buyer is interested in making an offer on the seller's property. Can this occur?

   1. No, because the real estate company would then be a dual agent
   2. Yes, as long as written agency agreements have been entered into with both parties
   3. Yes, if the seller has agreed to pay the commission
   4. Yes, if the buyer and seller both give their informed consent to dual agency

3. A seller's listing agreement has expired, and the seller lists with a different brokerage firm. The original listing agent now has a buyer interested in the seller's property. The original listing agent

   1. is a dual agent.
   2. cannot disclose to the buyer offers received on the seller's property while it was listed with him.
   3. cannot disclose to the buyer information about the physical condition of the property.
   4. cannot represent the buyer.

4. A real estate salesperson has been working with buyers. After helping them negotiate for their dream home, the buyers ask the salesperson if she can help them secure a mortgage. The salesperson knows a lender that pays a fee for referring purchasers to them. Can the salesperson refer the buyers to this lender and receive a referral fee?

   1. No, because a real estate licensee may not receive any type of referral fee for the referral of any buyer to a mortgage lender
   2. Yes, if the salesperson and the buyers have previously entered into a written buyer agency agreement
   3. Yes, if the salesperson discloses the referral fee to the sellers
   4. Yes, if the lender offers the market's best interest rates and terms

5. A buyer contacts a real estate office and indicates an interest in purchasing a home in the area. Without entering into a buyer agency relationship with the buyer, a salesperson from the real estate office can do all of the following EXCEPT

   1. provide the buyer with information on properties for sale in the area.
   2. give the buyer information on mortgage interest rates and terms.
   3. prequalify the buyer for a mortgage.
   4. explain to the buyer about buyer agency, seller agency, and dual agency.

6. A buyer prospect is interested in seeing a house listed with a real estate company, but does not wish to enter into a buyer agency agreement. A salesperson from the real estate company can show the buyer an in-house listing if the

1. salesperson obtains the seller's permission.
2. buyer verbally agrees to buyer agency.
3. salesperson provides the buyer with an agency disclosure notice that states the real estate company represents the seller.
4. salesperson provides the buyer with a dual agency consent form.

7. In Connecticut, an exclusive-right-to-buy contract

1. is illegal.
2. is equivalent to a listing agreement.
3. must be identified as such in the buyer agency agreement.
4. requires the signature of the principal only.

8. Buyer-brokerage contracts in Connecticut

1. must be in writing to be enforceable.
2. must be on specific forms.
3. are not regulated under the license laws.
4. are illegal.

9. All of the following provisions are included in the Connecticut Real Estate Commission's rules regarding listing agreements EXCEPT that a listing agreement must

1. identify the compensation to be paid to the broker.
2. be accompanied by a qualified expert's report of the property's condition.
3. be in writing and signed by both the broker and the seller.
4. contain a statement regarding brokers' lien rights.

10. All of the following types of agency are allowed in Connecticut EXCEPT

1. dual agency.
2. buyer's agency.
3. transaction agency.
4. subagency.

11. In a dual agency situation, a broker may collect a commission from both the seller and the buyer if

1. the broker holds a state license.
2. the buyer and the seller are related by blood or marriage.
3. both parties give their informed consent to the dual compensation.
4. both parties are represented by attorneys.

12. A buyer is interested in seeing a house listed with XYZ Realty but does not wish to enter into an agency relationship. A salesperson from LMN Realty can show the buyer the house if

   1. XYZ Realty obtains the seller's written consent to subagency, and the buyer is given an agency disclosure notice stating that LMN Realty represents the seller.
   2. XYZ Realty obtains LMN Realty's consent to subagency, and the buyer is given an agency disclosure notice stating that XYZ Realty represents the seller.
   3. the buyer verbally agrees to buyer agency.
   4. This cannot occur.

13. A seller is required to give a buyer a property condition disclosure report in all of the following transactions EXCEPT

   1. when the seller is not assisted by a licensed real estate agent.
   2. if the seller has not resided on the property in the last year.
   3. for a sale of commercial property.
   4. if the buyer has lived on the property as a tenant.

14. Seller property condition disclosure reports must be delivered to the buyer

   1. prior to the buyer making a written offer.
   2. at the time that the seller agrees to the offer.
   3. at the time of the home inspection.
   4. prior to closing.

15. A seller has no knowledge of any plumbing system problems on the property she is selling. In actuality, however, the pipes are seriously corroded and will need to be replaced soon. In the seller property condition disclosure report, when responding to whether the seller has any knowledge of plumbing system problems, she should respond

   1. "yes."
   2. "no."
   3. "unknown."
   4. The seller would not be required to respond to this question.

16. In Connecticut, when a broker is listing a home and asks the seller to complete a property condition disclosure report, which of the following statements is true?

   1. The disclosures are optional, and the seller may avoid liability by refusing to make any disclosures about the condition of the property.
   2. The standard disclosures cover a narrow range of structural conditions only.
   3. An agent should not give the seller any advice regarding which property conditions to disclose and which to ignore.
   4. Seller disclosure of known property conditions is required by Connecticut statute.

17. The salesperson represents the seller in a transaction. When prospective buyers ask to look at the property, the salesperson must

    1. tell them that they must first enter into a buyer representation agreement with another licensee.
    2. inform them in writing that the salesperson represents the seller's interests.
    3. inform them, either orally or in writing, that the salesperson represents the seller's interests.
    4. show them the property without making any disclosures about the salesperson's relationship with the seller because such disclosure would be a violation of the salesperson's fiduciary duties.

18. Five years ago, Unit 5B in a condominium community was the site of a brutal and highly publicized murder. The unit was then sold to an elderly woman who contracted the AIDS virus in a blood transfusion and died in the unit last year. As the agent for the woman's estate, what are your disclosure responsibilities to prospective purchasers of Unit 5B?

    1. You must disclose both the murder and the AIDS-related death.
    2. You are specifically prohibited by law from disclosing either event.
    3. You are specifically relieved of liability for nondisclosure of either event by the Connecticut license law.
    4. You do not need to disclose the murder, but you must disclose the AIDS-related death.

19. A broker took a listing for a small office building. Because the property is in excellent condition and produces a good, steady income, the broker's salesperson has decided to purchase it as an investment. If the broker's salesperson wishes to buy this property, the salesperson must

    1. resign as the broker's agent and make an offer after the owner has retained another broker.
    2. have a third party purchase the property on the salesperson's behalf so that the owner does not learn the true identity of the purchaser.
    3. obtain permission from the Connecticut Real Estate Commission.
    4. inform the owner in writing that the salesperson is a licensee in the broker's office before making an offer.

20. Six months after a buyer bought a house, the roof leaked during a rainstorm. When the house was listed, the seller told the broker that the roof leaked, but they agreed not to tell any prospective buyers. The broker claims that the buyer did not ask about the roof. Under these facts, the buyer

    1. can sue the broker for nondisclosure.
    2. cannot sue the broker under the license law.
    3. can sue the seller under license law.
    4. cannot do anything because the leaking roof could have been discovered by inspection.

21. When must a real estate licensee representing the seller give the agency disclosure notice to a prospective purchaser that is represented by another brokerage firm?

    1. Before the purchaser is shown any properties
    2. At an open house
    3. Before any offer to purchase is prepared or presented
    4. Never

22. A real estate licensee has signed a brokerage agreement with a tenant who is looking for an apartment to rent. The licensee does not charge a fee to prospective tenants; rather, the licensee receives a commission from landlords. The licensee tells a landlord that the prospective tenant could pay a higher rent than the landlord is asking. Which of the following statements is true?

    1. The licensee owes the statutory agency duties to the landlords who pay the commission.
    2. The licensee's disclosure to the landlord was appropriate under these circumstances.
    3. The licensee's disclosure violated the statutory duties owed to the tenant.
    4. Because the licensee is not charging a fee to prospective tenants, the licensee has violated Connecticut agency statute.

23. All of the following types of transfers are excluded from the property condition disclosure law EXCEPT a

    1. foreclosure sale.
    2. gift of property by a grandfather to his granddaughter.
    3. conveyance of an interest in a primary residence from one owner/spouse to the other owner/spouse under a divorce settlement agreement.
    4. sale by a real estate licensee of a two-unit apartment building.

24. A licensed salesperson obtains a listing. Several days later, the salesperson meets an unrepresented prospective buyer at the property and tells her, "I am the listing agent for this property, and so I'm very familiar with it." Under these circumstances, the salesperson

    1. has failed to properly disclose his or her agency relationship.
    2. has properly disclosed his or her agency relationship with the seller.
    3. is in violation of Connecticut regulations since the listing belongs to the broker.
    4. has created a dual agency, which is a violation of Connecticut regulations.

25. A real estate broker representing the seller knows that the property has a cracked foundation and that its former owner committed suicide in the kitchen. The broker must disclose

    1. both facts.
    2. the suicide, but not the cracked foundation.
    3. the cracked foundation, but not the suicide.
    4. neither fact.

26. A broker has entered into a listing agreement with the seller. Another broker, who has been working with a buyer, learns of the property through the MLS. Typically the second, cooperating broker would represent

    1. the seller as a subagent.
    2. the buyer as an agent.
    3. the buyer as a subagent.
    4. neither the buyer nor seller.

27. When a broker represents the seller of real estate, an agency disclosure must be given to the

    1. seller, at the beginning of the first personal meeting with the seller concerning the real estate.
    2. seller, at the time the listing agreement is signed.
    3. purchaser, before the purchase and sale contract is signed.
    4. unrepresented purchaser, at the beginning of the first personal meeting with the purchaser.

28. A realty company has entered into agency agreements with both a seller and a buyer. The seller and the buyer have signed the dual agency consent agreement. The salesperson with the realty company that has been working with the buyer may

    1. provide comparable market data to the seller, after the buyer requests and receives such data from the salesperson.
    2. disclose the buyer's financial qualifications the seller.
    3. disclose to the buyer that the seller will accept less than the listing price.
    4. disclose to the seller that the buyer will pay more than the offering price.

29. A broker decides to "sweeten" an MLS listing for a property by making a blanket offer of subagency. Is the broker's action acceptable?

    1. Yes, because Connecticut law permits the creation of subagency relationships only through multiple-listing services
    2. Yes, because a subagency relationship may be created by either a blanket offer in an MLS or through a specific agreement between parties
    3. No, because subagency is illegal under Connecticut law
    4. No, because subagency relationships in Connecticut may be created only with specific consent of the seller

30. A buyer who is a client of a broker wants to purchase a house that the broker has listed for sale. Which of the following statements is true?

    1. If the listing salesperson and selling salesperson are two different people, there is no problem.
    2. The broker should refer the buyer to another broker to negotiate the sale.
    3. The seller and buyer must be informed of the situation and agree to the broker's representation of both of them.
    4. The buyer should not have been shown a house listed by the broker.

31. A brokerage firm represents both the buyer and the seller. The seller does not wish to work with a salesperson who is a dual agent. Which of the following statements is true?

    1. The seller must agree to dual agency, since he has entered into an agency agreement with the firm.
    2. The broker must refer the buyer to another brokerage to negotiate the sale.
    3. Salespeople are never dual agents, only the designated broker is.
    4. The broker can designate one salesperson to be the agent of the seller and another to be the agent of the buyer; in this case the salespeople would not be dual agents.

32. A broker represents a seller in a transaction. The broker introduces a buyer to the property, and the buyer and seller sign a purchase and sales contract. The seller has indicated that he does not feel that a commission is owed the broker, when in fact the broker is entitled to a commission. To secure compensation for her services, the broker may place a lien in the land records

    1. prior to the conveyance.
    2. within 30 days of the conveyance.
    3. prior to the expiration of the listing agreement.
    4. never; a broker is not allowed to place a lien on property.

33. In Connecticut, real estate commissions

    1. are always six percent of the purchase price.
    2. must be between three and six percent of the purchase price, depending on whether there is one or more than one real estate licensee involved.
    3. vary throughout the state, as determined by local groups of brokers.
    4. are negotiable between the seller/buyer and the broker.

34. A real estate broker enters into a written listing agreement to list a seller's home in Connecticut. The next weekend, the broker holds an open house at the seller's house to show the property to prospective purchasers. A buyer comes to the open house and asks the broker if there are other houses in the neighborhood for sale. As of this point, and based on the above facts, which of the following is true?

    1. Both the seller and the buyer are the broker's clients.
    2. The seller is the broker's client; the buyer is a customer.
    3. It is illegal for the broker to represent both the seller and the buyer, as the broker would then be a dual agent.
    4. The broker must designate one salesperson to represent the seller and another to represent the buyer.

35. The basement in a seller's house regularly floods when it rains heavily. The seller does not feel that this is a material fact since his basement is unfinished. While he does tell his real estate agent about the problem, he also states that he would be disappointed if a potential purchaser did not consider the house because of it. Given this scenario, the agent

    1. should not disclose the flooding problem to potential purchasers, as the agent would then violate his or her fiduciary duty to the seller.
    2. is not required to disclose the flooding problem since the agent has no firsthand knowledge of it.
    3. should only discuss the flooding problem to potential purchasers who ask about it.
    4. must disclose the flooding problem to potential purchasers.

36. A broker listed a seller's house for $199,000. The seller's job has recently been relocated, so he confides in the broker that he must sell the house quickly and that he would consider taking a lower price. To expedite the sale, the broker tells a prospective purchaser that seller will accept up to $10,000 less than the asking price for the property. Based on these facts, which of the following statements is true?

    1. The broker's disclosure violated his or her fiduciary duty to the seller.
    2. The broker's disclosure was necessitated by his or her duty of full disclosure to prospective purchasers, only if such disclosure was a material fact.
    3. The broker's disclosure was necessitated by his or her duty of full disclosure to prospective purchasers, regardless of whether such disclosure was a material fact.
    4. The broker can only make this type of disclosure if it is for the purpose of expediting the sale.

37. At an open house, a prospective buyer asks the real estate broker if the broker can show her other houses for sale in the neighborhood. The prospective buyer, however, is reluctant to enter into a buyer agency agreement. Can the broker show the prospective buyer other houses, without entering into such an agreement?

    1. No, the broker can only work with the prospective buyer as a client.
    2. No, since the prospective buyer came to an open house, the broker must not show her any other properties.
    3. Yes, the broker can work with the prospective buyer as a client without a written agreement.
    4. Yes, the broker can show the prospective buyer other houses that her firm has listings on, in which case the broker will represent the sellers of those houses, not the prospective buyer.

38. If a broker represents a seller of a house that a customer of the broker is interested in, an agency disclosure notice must be given to the

    1. seller, at the beginning of the first personal meeting concerning the real estate.
    2. seller, at the time the listing agreement is signed.
    3. prospective buyer, at the beginning of the broker's first personal meeting with him or her.
    4. prospective buyer, before any purchase and sale agreement is signed.

39. A prospective purchaser decides to enter into an agency relationship with a real estate broker. The agreement includes the following language: "In return for the compensation agreed upon, Broker will assist Client in locating and purchasing a suitable property. Broker will receive the agreed upon compensation regardless of whether Broker, Client, or some other party locates the property ultimately purchased by Client." What kind of agreement is this?

    1. Exclusive-agency listing
    2. Exclusive-agency buyer agency agreement
    3. Exclusive buyer agency agreement
    4. Open buyer agency agreement

40. A real estate broker has entered into an agency agreement with both a seller and a prospective buyer. The prospective buyer is now interested in making an offer on the seller's property. Can this occur?

    1. No, because the broker would then be a dual agent
    2. Yes, as long as the broker has entered into written agency agreements with both the seller and the buyer
    3. Yes, if the seller has agreed to pay the commission
    4. Yes, if, in addition to both the seller and the buyer having entered into written agency agreements with the broker, both the seller and the buyer give their informed consent to dual agency

41. A real estate broker has entered into an agency agreement with both a seller and a buyer. The buyer is now interested in making an offer on the seller's property, but is uncomfortable working with the broker since she also represents the seller. Must the buyer be referred to another real estate brokerage firm?

    1. Yes, there are no other agency options.
    2. No, the broker can elect designated agency, rather than dual agency status.
    3. No, the broker's firm can designate one salesperson to represent the buyer and another to represent the seller, in which case neither salesperson would be a dual agent.
    4. No, the broker is permitted to proceed as a dual agent as long as one of the parties consents.

42. In Connecticut, the real estate license law is administered by the

    1. Connecticut Commission on Human Rights and Opportunities.
    2. Connecticut Real Estate Commission.
    3. Connecticut Association of REALTORS®.
    4. Department of Housing and Urban Development (HUD).

43. How are members of the Connecticut Real Estate Commission selected?

    1. By the governor
    2. Public election
    3. By the state association of REALTORS®
    4. Elected by real estate licensees

44. In Connecticut, which of the following would need to be a licensed real estate broker or salesperson?

    1. An apartment leasing agent employed by an owner of an apartment complex
    2. A licensed attorney serving as legal counsel to his or her client
    3. A resident apartment manager working for an owner if the manager's primary residence is the apartment building being managed
    4. A non-real estate business partnership selling a building owned by the partners

45. Which of the following requires a real estate license?

    1. Resident manager who collects rent on behalf of a building owner
    2. Company that, for a fee (not a commission), matches individuals from different parts of the country who want to exchange properties and that assists them in doing so
    3. Employee of nonprofit housing corporation who manages a Section 8 housing project
    4. Executor selling a decedent's building

46. Under Connecticut law, any person who acts as a real property securities dealer must

    1. hold a Connecticut real estate license.
    2. have his or her securities license endorsed by the Connecticut Real Estate Commission.
    3. be approved by the SEC.
    4. There are no special licensing requirements for real property securities dealers.

47. Under Connecticut licensing law, a partnership, association, or corporation will be granted a real estate license only if

    1. the firm's designated broker retains a current license.
    2. every officer and employee actively participating in the brokerage business has a broker's license.
    3. all papers are filed with the secretary of state.
    4. the brokerage business has paid a one-time fee to the guaranty fund.

48. A real estate license is required for all of the following activities EXCEPT

    1. managing real estate.
    2. reselling a mobile home.
    3. selling real estate.
    4. renting real estate on behalf of a resident landlord.

49. If engaged in real estate activities, which of the following are exempt from the real estate licensing requirement?

    1. Attorneys at law when serving as legal counsel to their clients
    2. Appraisers
    3. Associations, partnerships, corporations
    4. Real property securities dealers

50. The office manager for a local real estate firm is responsible for the following activities: coordinating the flow of paperwork through the office, preparing forms and advertising copy, and hiring and supervising clerical personnel. The office manager is

    1. violating the license law.
    2. required to have a broker's license.
    3. required to have a salesperson's license.
    4. exempt from real estate licensing requirements.

51. In Connecticut, applications for any real estate license must

    1. be completed before taking the written exam.
    2. contain a picture of the applicant.
    3. be made before May 31 of each year.
    4. be accompanied by a sworn statement attesting to the applicant's character.

52. In Connecticut, all of the following are requirements for obtaining a broker's license EXCEPT

    1. having successfully completed 90 hours of approved real estate courses.
    2. being at least 18 years of age.
    3. having been actively engaged as a licensed salesperson for at least three years.
    4. submitting letters of character reference.

53. Three weeks before N begins his real estate prelicense class, he offers to help his neighbor sell her house. The neighbor agrees to pay N a five percent commission. An offer is accepted while N is taking the class and closes the day before N passes the examination and receives his salesperson's license. The neighbor refuses to pay N the agreed commission. Can N sue to recover payment?

    1. Yes, N was formally enrolled in a course of study intended to result in a real estate license at the time an offer was procured and accepted, and therefore the commission agreement is binding.
    2. No, in Connecticut, a real estate salesperson must have a permanent office in which his or her license is displayed in order to collect a commission from a seller.
    3. Yes, while the statute of frauds forbids recovery on an oral agreement for the conveyance of real property, Connecticut law permits enforcement of an oral commission contract under these facts.
    4. No, state law prohibits lawsuits to collect commissions unless the injured party is a licensed broker and the license was in effect at the time the real estate services were rendered.

54. An applicant for a real estate license in Connecticut must

    1. have completed at least two years of college.
    2. be at least 21 years old.
    3. not have been convicted of a felony within five years before applying.
    4. show proof of passing the license examination.

55. An unlicensed individual who engages in activities for which a real estate license is required is subject to which of the following penalties?

    1. Fine not to exceed $5,000
    2. Fine not to exceed $1,000 and/or imprisonment up to than six months
    3. Civil penalty of $5,000
    4. Civil penalty not to exceed $5,000 and a mandatory prison term not to exceed five years

56. When do real estate salespersons' licenses expire in Connecticut?

    1. March 31 of every even-numbered year
    2. January 1 annually
    3. May 31 annually
    4. May 31 of every even-numbered year

57. To renew a license in Connecticut, a salesperson or broker must

    1. pay a fee of $225 only.
    2. be actively participating in the real estate business.
    3. have completed six hours of continuing education in the last two years, three hours in real estate law and three hours in fair housing.
    4. pay a fee of $225 annually and in even-numbered years have completed 12 hours of continuing education in the last two years.

58. In Connecticut, licenses are renewed

    1. annually, in the month issued.
    2. every two years in the month of the licensee's birthday.
    3. on June 30 of each even-numbered year.
    4. on May 31 of each year.

59. What continuing education requirements must be met by salespersons?

    1. 3 hours of law/fair housing update; 9 hours of other approved CE every year
    2. 3 hours of law/fair housing update; 9 hours of other approved CE every two years
    3. 12 hours in listing, buying, and ethics every two years
    4. There are no mandatory requirements.

60. In Connecticut, an unlicensed real estate assistant may perform all of the following activities EXCEPT

    1. compute commission checks.
    2. assemble legal documents required for a closing.
    3. explain simple contract documents to prospective buyers.
    4. prepare and distribute flyers and promotional materials.

61. Personal real estate assistants in Connecticut

    1. must be licensed.
    2. may type contract forms under the employing broker's supervision and approval.
    3. may independently host open houses and home show booths.
    4. must be unlicensed individuals; licensees must be either salespeople or associate brokers.

62. A broker's unlicensed assistant worked late nights and weekends to help ensure the successful closing of a difficult transaction. The assistant's extra work included making several phone calls to the prospective buyers, encouraging them to accept the seller's counteroffer. Largely because of the assistant's efforts, the sale went through with no problem. Now the broker wants to pay the assistant a percentage of the commission, "because the assistant has really earned it." Under Connecticut law, the

    1. broker may compensate the assistant in the form of a commission under the circumstances described here.
    2. personal assistant may sue for a greater commission.
    3. broker and personal assistant are both in violation of rules regarding unlicensed assistants.
    4. broker may pay a commission to the assistant only if the assistant is an independent contractor.

63. If a person obtains a Connecticut reciprocal real estate license, he or she must

    1. pass a written exam.
    2. establish a principal place of business in Connecticut.
    3. take all education course requirements in Connecticut.
    4. file an irrevocable consent to suit agreement with the Connecticut Real Estate Commission.

64. A nonresident license applicant must file with the commission a(n)

    1. certificate of specific performance.
    2. irrevocable consent to suit.
    3. copy of his or her birth certificate.
    4. corpus delicti.

65. An individual wants to sell her own house. Which of the following statements is true?

    1. She does not need a real estate license to sell her house herself.
    2. In Connecticut, anyone who sells real property must first have a real estate license issued by the commission.
    3. The individual may obtain a temporary real estate license in order to legally sell her house.
    4. She may sell her house without obtaining a real estate license only if she has hired a licensed attorney.

66. Which of the following is a requirement to obtain a real estate salesperson's license in Connecticut?

    1. Successful completion of 12 credit hours of real estate law and fair housing
    2. An associate degree or certificate in real estate from an accredited college, university, or proprietary school
    3. United States and Connecticut citizenship
    4. Successful completion of a 30 hour course of an approved real estate principles and practice course

67. All Connecticut real estate licenses

    1. are granted in perpetuity.
    2. do not need to be renewed unless previously revoked.
    3. expire annually on April 30.
    4. expire annually on May 31.

68. A person must be licensed as a real estate broker or salesperson if that person is

    1. selling his or her house.
    2. helping a friend buy a house free of charge.
    3. helping a friend sell his or her home for a small fee.
    4. constructing houses.

69. Who may receive compensation from the real estate guaranty fund?

    1. Broker who unjustly does not receive her earned commission
    2. Buyer who is contractually obligated to pay a fee to a broker, even though the house the buyer bought was sold by the owner directly
    3. Cooperating broker who does not receive a commission split
    4. Seller who paid a commission to a broker after the broker fraudulently stated that a buyer for the seller's property had been found

70. The Connecticut Real Estate Commission can revoke a licensee's license in all of the following scenarios EXCEPT when a

    1. salesperson enthusiastically tells a buyer that a parcel of real estate is two acres, when the salesperson knows that it is only one acre.
    2. broker is acting as a dual agent, with the informed consent of all the parties involved.
    3. broker enters into an exclusive-listing agreement with a seller that expires in three months, with an automatic one-month extension.
    4. salesperson, without the consent of her broker, moonlights for another non-competing brokerage firm.

71. A broker or salesperson whose license has been revoked by the Connecticut Real Estate Commission can appeal the commission decision to the

    1. Connecticut Department of Consumer Protection.
    2. governor's office.
    3. Real Estate Disciplinary Board.
    4. Hartford-New Britain Superior Court.

72. In Connecticut, all of the following would be grounds for revoking a broker's license EXCEPT

    1. being convicted of a felony.
    2. failing to immediately deliver a copy of a listing agreement to the seller that signed it.
    3. depositing escrow money in his or her personal checking account.
    4. agreeing with a seller to accept a listing for more than the normal commission rate.

73. The commission has the power to revoke a salesperson's license if the salesperson

    1. attempts to represent a real estate broker other than his or her employing broker, after obtaining the employer's consent.
    2. attempts to represent a buyer.
    3. enters into an exclusive-listing contract.
    4. deposits a buyer's down payment in his or her personal bank account.

74. In Connecticut, a broker may have his or her license suspended or revoked for all of the following actions EXCEPT

    1. failing to give a proper agency disclosure notice to an unrepresented party.
    2. depositing earnest money into the firm's escrow account.
    3. helping another person cheat on the licensing examination.
    4. displaying a "For Sale" sign on a property without the owner's consent.

75. If a broker tells a lender that the sales price on a property is something above its actual sales price, the

    1. broker has done nothing wrong as long as the appraisal substantiates this price.
    2. buyer is likely to receive an interest rate break.
    3. broker can lose his or her license and be fined and imprisoned.
    4. buyer can receive a higher mortgage amount.

76. Salesperson Janet paid a telephone company to list her name in the directory under the real estate heading as "Janet, Real Estate Salesperson, Residential Property My Specialty." Based on this information, Janet must also include

    1. her license number.
    2. the expiration date of her license.
    3. her street address.
    4. the name of her employing broker.

77. A broker who wishes to place a "For Sale" sign on a listed property must first

    1. obtain the consent of the owner of the property.
    2. sell the property.
    3. list the property.
    4. get permission from the neighbors.

78. When advertising real property, real estate licensees

    1. may state only the licensee's box number or street address.
    2. may simply give a telephone number to call for more information.
    3. must indicate that the ads were placed in the name of a licensed real estate broker.
    4. must identify the owner of the property.

79. A real estate salesperson decides to sell his or her own property without using a broker. When advertising the property, the salesperson

    1. must disclose the name, address, and phone number of his or her employing broker.
    2. must disclose the fact that he or she is a real estate licensee.
    3. does not need to disclose licensed status if acting as a private citizen.
    4. is prohibited from selling his or her own home in this manner by license law.

80. Listings based on a "net price" are

    1. more profitable because no minimum is set on the amount of commission collectible.
    2. legal in Connecticut as long as the seller agrees.
    3. illegal in Connecticut at any time.
    4. permissible with approval of the commission.

81. A seller told a broker that she wanted to clear $50,000 when she sold her house. The broker accepted the listing and sold it for $160,000. He gave $50,000 to the seller and kept the rest. Which of the following is correct?

    1. The broker should have given the seller a better appraisal of the value of her house.
    2. The broker's commission exceeds statutory and NAR guidelines.
    3. The broker accepted an illegal net listing.
    4. As the seller's agent, the broker had a duty to sell the house for as much as possible.

82. In Connecticut, real estate commissions are

   1. set by law.
   2. set by the Connecticut Real Estate Commission.
   3. determined by local groups of brokers.
   4. negotiable between the seller and buyer and broker.

83. Commissions earned by a broker in a real estate sales transaction

   1. are determined by agreement of the broker and his or her principal.
   2. may be shared with an unlicensed person, provided that such person aided the broker in bringing the buyer and seller together.
   3. may be deducted from the earnest money deposit and claimed by the broker as soon as the buyer and seller execute the purchase and sales agreement.
   4. are based on a schedule of commission rates set by the Connecticut Real Estate Commission.

84. All funds received by a broker on behalf of his or her principal must be deposited in an escrow or trust account within

   1. three days of receiving the offer.
   2. three banking days of obtaining all signatures for the contract.
   3. five working days of receiving the offer.
   4. five banking days of receiving all signatures.

85. A broker received an earnest money deposit from a buyer of $9,000. Under Connecticut law, the broker should

   1. deposit the money in a special interest-bearing escrow account, where interest is directed to be paid to a government authority.
   2. deposit the money in a special non-interest-bearing escrow.
   3. immediately (or by the next business day) deposit the earnest money in the broker's personal interest-bearing checking or savings account, where interest is directed to be paid to the broker.
   4. hold the earnest money deposit in a secure place in the broker's real estate brokerage office until the offer is accepted.

86. A broker received a buyer's earnest money check for $5,000 and immediately cashed it. At closing, the broker handed the seller a personal check drawn on his own bank account for $5,300, representing the original earnest money plus six percent interest. The broker

   1. should have deposited the money in a special non-interest-bearing bank account.
   2. properly cashed the check, but should have kept the interest
   3. should have deposited the money in his personal bank account, and would have been entitled to keep the interest as a service fee.
   4. should have deposited the money in a special bank account, and should have discussed the interest with the parties.

87. All of the following must appear in a written listing agreement EXCEPT

   1. a statement that the broker's compensation is not fixed by law and is negotiable.
   2. the complete legal description of the property being sold.
   3. the expiration date of the agreement.
   4. a statement acknowledging adherence to the Connecticut statutes pertaining to fair housing.

88. A broker signs a listing agreement with a seller. The agreement contains the following clause: "If the Property has not been sold after three months from the date of this signing, this agreement will automatically continue for additional three-month periods thereafter until the property is sold." Based on these facts, the agreement

   1. is legal under Connecticut law, because it contains a reference to a specific time limit.
   2. is illegal in Connecticut.
   3. would automatically rollover or be extended until the property in sold.
   4. is legal under Connecticut law, because the list periods are for less than six months each.

89. Regarding listing agreements in Connecticut, which of the following could result in the suspension or revocation of a licensee's license to practice real estate?

   1. A specified commission rate
   2. No specific termination date
   3. No broker protection clause
   4. A specific termination date

90. Upon obtaining a listing, a broker or licensed salesperson is obligated to

   1. set up a listing file and issue it a number in compliance with Connecticut real estate license law and rules.
   2. place advertisements in the local newspapers.
   3. cooperate with every real estate office wishing to participate in the marketing of the listed property.
   4. give the person or persons signing the listing an executed copy.

91. A seller listed his house for sale with a broker on February 1. The listing agreement was to last five months. In April, the seller decided that the house was no longer for sale. Which of the following statements is true?

   1. The seller has canceled the agreement and there are no penalties.
   2. The seller has withdrawn the broker's authority to sell the property and may be subject to a penalty.
   3. The seller is required by law to leave his house on the market until June.
   4. The Connecticut Real Estate Commission will decide if the seller's action is justifiable.

92. A person who believes that he or she has been illegally discriminated against in violation of fair housing laws may file a complaint with the Connecticut

   1. Board of REALTORS®.
   2. Attorney General.
   3. Real Estate Commission.
   4. Commission on Human Rights and Opportunities or HUD.

93. A housing discrimination charge must be filed with the Connecticut Commission on Human Rights and Opportunities within

    1. 3 months.
    2. 180 days.
    3. 1 year.
    4. 30 days.

94. A landlord is interested in renting a condominium unit strictly by word of mouth, without advertising and without the use of an agent. A single man in his late sixties who is confined to a wheelchair, is interested in renting the condo, but must be allowed to build a ramp to access the entrance. The landlord will rent to the tenant, but insists that the tenant build the ramp at his own expense and remove it when his lease expires. Is the tenant being discriminated against?

    1. Yes, the landlord is required to allow the tenant to modify the apartment and to pay for the modifications.
    2. Yes, all rental residences are required to be handicapped accessible, and this one is not.
    3. No, the landlord is under no obligation to accommodate the tenant.
    4. No, the landlord is only required to allow the tenant to modify the apartment, but is not required to pay for the modifications.

95. If a buyer wants to have a clause included in the sales contract under which the seller offers assurances against the existence of werewolves, vampires, and trolls on the property, which of the following statements is true in Connecticut?

    1. The broker may include the clause, because such standard supernatural disclosures are in general usage.
    2. Only a licensed attorney may prepare the clause for inclusion in the sales contract.
    3. In Connecticut, brokers are permitted to add additional clauses to blank form contracts, such as the clause described here, that do not directly involve the conveyance of title to real property.
    4. Under Connecticut law, a frivolous clause, such as the one described here, is not permitted and any contract containing such a clause will be invalid.

96. A Connecticut real estate salesperson may lawfully collect compensation from

    1. either a buyer or a seller.
    2. his or her employing broker only.
    3. any party to the transaction or the party's representative.
    4. a licensed real estate broker only.

97. What are the procedures that a salesperson must follow when the salesperson decides to change his or her employment from one broker to another?

    1. Give the broker an official letter of termination that he or she can send to the Connecticut Real Estate Commission
    2. Nothing; the broker is responsible for notifying the Connecticut Real Estate Commission of the change
    3. Register the change with the Connecticut Real Estate Commission and pay a $25 fee
    4. Return his or her license, along with a letter of termination, to the Connecticut Real Estate Commission

98. A licensed salesperson may hold a concurrent license with more than one Connecticut broker under which of the following circumstances?

    1. Under no circumstances
    2. With the permission of his or her sales manager
    3. With the written consent of the brokers being represented
    4. With the permission of the Connecticut Real Estate Commission

99. Several weeks after a closing, an associate broker received a thank you letter and a nice bonus check from the seller of a house. The associate broker cashed the check because he felt it was earned. In this situation, which of the following is true?

    1. The associate broker may accept the bonus because he is licensed as an associate broker.
    2. Accepting the money is allowed if more than 30 days have elapsed since the closing.
    3. The associate broker may accept the money if his broker permits him to do so.
    4. Accepting the money is a violation of commission regulations.

100. An airline pilot told a broker about some friends who were looking for a new home. The broker contacted the friends and eventually sold them a house. When may the broker pay the airline pilot for this valuable lead?

    1. As soon as a valid sales contract is signed by the parties
    2. Only after the sale closes
    3. After the funds are released from escrow
    4. The broker may not pay the airline pilot for the lead.

101. Connecticut law prohibits a licensee from demanding a referral fee unless a reasonable cause for payment exists. A reasonable cause for payment would include all of the following EXCEPT the

    1. actual introduction of business.
    2. existence of a subagency relationship.
    3. existence of contractual referral fee relationship.
    4. relocation company policy requirement of such a fee in order to work with a broker.

102. The Connecticut Real Estate Commission has the right to suspend or revoke the license of a licensee that has been convicted of certain crimes. Who is required to notify the commission of such a conviction?

    1. Plaintiff or victim in any court case
    2. Clerk of the court in which the conviction takes place
    3. Convicted licensee's brokerage firm
    4. Convicted licensee

103. A buyer has just entered into a contract to buy a condominium unit from a person who originally bought the unit from the developer and has lived there for the past ten years. This new buyer has a right to cancel the contract within

    1. 5 business days of receipt of resale documents.
    2. 15 business days of receipt of resale documents.
    3. 5 days from the date of the newly executed contract.
    4. The new buyer does not have the right to cancel a signed contract in this situation.

104. How is a broker's commission determined in a real estate sales transaction?

    1. It must be stated in the listing agreement and is negotiated between the broker and seller.
    2. It is determined according to the standard rates set by agreement of local real estate brokers.
    3. If under dispute, it will be determined through arbitration by the Connecticut Real Estate Commission.
    4. It is set by the Connecticut Association of REALTORS®.

105. A broker has obtained an offer to purchase a residence that is listed with his firm. After the buyers sign a purchase and sale agreement and the broker accepts their earnest money deposit, the broker must

    1. deposit the earnest money in the broker's personal checking account for safekeeping until closing.
    2. complete a second earnest money agreement form that states an exaggerated selling price and give the second form to the buyers to present to the lender so that they will be certain to obtain sufficient financing for their purchase.
    3. immediately provide the buyers a copy of the agreement.
    4. file the agreement in the broker's records and, when two or three other offers have been received for the property, present them all to the sellers, who then may choose the best offer.

106. In Connecticut, the age of legal competence is

    1. 18.
    2. 19.
    3. 20.
    4. 21.

107. Which of the following is not a protected class under the Connecticut fair housing law?

    1. Familial status
    2. Disability
    3. Sexual preference
    4. Amount of income

108. In Connecticut, what is the statutory usury ceiling on loans secured by real estate?

    1. 10 percent
    2. 15 percent
    3. 22 percent
    4. There is none.

109. Unclaimed estates escheat to the state after a period of

    1. 5 years.
    2. 10 years.
    3. 15 years.
    4. 20 years.

110. A couple with a five-year-old son lives in their own home in Connecticut. Knowing their house contains some surfaces with lead paint, the couple had their son tested for evaluated blood levels, and the tests showed he had no lead in his system. Does Connecticut law require that the parents take any action with regard to the lead paint in their home?

    1. Yes, they must abate all lead paint.
    2. Yes, they must abate defective lead paint.
    3. No, as long as the boy does not have an elevated blood lead level, they need not conduct any abatement.
    4. No, abatement of lead paint is required only in rental housing.

111. A property owner discovers that there is an underground oil storage tank in her backyard. Which of the following situations would NOT apply to her situation?

    1. The owner may be required to remove the tank.
    2. The owner may be held liable for cleanup costs if the tank has leaked.
    3. The owner should not disclose the tank to a potential purchaser.
    4. If the owner recently purchased the property and the seller did not disclose that the tank was there, the new owner may be able to rescind the transaction.

112. How long before the signing of a sales contract for recreational lots outside Connecticut must the seller present a purchaser with a prospectus?

    1. 24 hours
    2. Within 72 hours
    3. Five business days
    4. One week

113. All of the following are title search methods commonly used by an attorney in Connecticut EXCEPT a

    1. land court certificate.
    2. title search and opinion.
    3. certificate of title.
    4. full abstract.

114. If a foreclosure sale fails to cover the outstanding loan amount owed, the lender can

    1. collect a deficiency judgment.
    2. refinance the property.
    3. have the borrower arrested.
    4. do nothing.

115. The purpose of the Connecticut Affordable Housing Land Use Appeals Act is to

    1. encourage the development of affordable housing in the state.
    2. secure adequate provision of housing services to low-income and moderate-income residents.
    3. establish construction standards for affordable housing.
    4. enforce a uniform zoning law that creates mandatory housing projects in higher-income areas.

116. A sales contract is signed on May 1. Closing takes place on June 10, and the deed is recorded on June 15. The borrower's first mortgage payment is due on August 30. When is the soonest that the broker receive his or her commission check?

    1. May 1
    2. June 10
    3. June 15
    4. August 30

117. In Connecticut, who is responsible prior to closing for calculating the prorations between the buyer and seller, searching the title, and preparing the mortgage note and deed?

    1. Broker
    2. Salesperson
    3. Closing attorney
    4. Lender

118. A broker or salesperson may perform all of the following in preparation for the closing EXCEPT

    1. maintain a time schedule and provide net data.
    2. explain closing procedures to both the buyer and the seller and anticipate decision-making alternatives.
    3. coordinate inspections and deliver documents and escrow monies to the appropriate attorney.
    4. conduct any title searches that might be required.

119. In Connecticut, who normally pays the property expenses for the day of closing?

    1. Seller
    2. Buyer
    3. Closing attorney
    4. Seller's broker

120. A husband is survived by his wife and their two daughters. The couple's jointly held property is worth $50,000, but the husband has also left a separate estate worth $150,000. Because the husband died suddenly without leaving a will, the wife

    1. acquires sole ownership of the jointly held property and her daughters each receive $75,000 from the husband's separate property.
    2. acquires sole ownership of all of the property.
    3. receives all $50,000 of the jointly held property and $125,000 from the husband's separate property, and her daughters each receive $12,500.
    4. receives one-half of the entire estate or $25,000 from the jointly held property and $75,000 from the husband's separate property, while her daughters each receive one-half of the balance of the entire estate or $50,000.

121. A nephew was a witness to his uncle's will. When the will was read after the uncle's death, the nephew discovered that he was a devisee of his uncle's will. Which of the following statements is true?

    1. Because the nephew is a witness, the nephew's devise may be void.
    2. As a witness, the nephew should have read the will.
    3. Because the nephew is a witness, the will is void.
    4. The nephew has a right of election.

122. A decedent left an estate valued at $800,000, after the payment of all taxes and debts. She had no surviving husband, but three children. The first son died shortly after his mother did, leaving two children, one of whom is adopted. The daughter has three children and the remaining son has two. The decedent did not write a will. How is her property divided?

    1. The daughter and remaining son each take $400,000.
    2. The daughter and the remaining son each take $266,666, and the first son's children each take $133,333.
    3. The daughter takes $342,857, the remaining son takes $228,571, and each of the first son's children takes $114,285.
    4. The estate will escheat to the state.

123. How old must a citizen of Connecticut be before he or she may prepare a legally binding will?

    1. 15
    2. 18
    3. 21
    4. Any age as long as the will is legally witnessed and recorded

124. How many witnesses must sign in the presence of the person making a will to fulfill the legal minimum?

    1. One
    2. Two
    3. Three
    4. Four

125. Which of the following legal life estates could be available to a surviving husband in Connecticut?

    1. Statutory survivorship rights
    2. Dower
    3. Curtesy
    4. Homestead

126. The purpose of homestead is to

    1. protect spouses against disinheritance.
    2. ensure the payment of taxes, claims, and liens.
    3. protect a person's equity in his or her home.
    4. permit a surviving spouse to retain the home.

127. A husband and wife are residents of Connecticut. If their co-owned home is sold in order to satisfy their unpaid credit card debts, how much will the creditors receive if the property sells for $165,000?

    1. Nothing. By statute in Connecticut, a resident's home may not be sold except to satisfy a mortgage debt or real estate taxes.
    2. $90,000
    3. $150,000
    4. $163,600

128. A single parent has three young children. The parent's house is worth $75,000. What is the total maximum value of the homestead exemption?

    1. $5,000
    2. $6,500
    3. $70,000
    4. $75,000

129. The principal method of delineating property boundaries or legal descriptions in Connecticut is known as the

    1. colonial block grant system.
    2. system of principal meridians and base lines.
    3. system of metes and bounds.
    4. rectangular survey system.

130. A homeowner's property has an iron pin located on the corner point of the lot. This pin serves the same function as a

    1. base point.
    2. fence post.
    3. map.
    4. monument.

131. A homeowner contracted with ABC Construction Company to put a new deck on her house. They began work on May 1 and finished on June 1, but they were never paid. On July 1, The homeowner sold her house to a buyer, who received a mortgage loan from Country Bank and a mortgage loan from City Bank. City Bank recorded its mortgage on July 1. Country Bank recorded its mortgage on July 2. ABC Construction Company records a mechanic's lien on July 3. What is the priority of the liens?

    1. ABC Construction, City Bank, Country Bank
    2. City Bank, Country Bank, ABC Construction
    3. ABC Construction, then City Bank and Country Bank equally
    4. City Bank and Country Bank equally, then ABC Construction

132. For three days, a property owner watched from his kitchen window as a small construction crew built an attractive gazebo in his back yard. The owner had not contracted with anyone to build a gazebo and in fact had never given much thought to having one. But the homeowner liked what he saw. When the contractor presented the homeowner with a bill for the work, the homeowner refused to pay pointing out that he'd never signed a contract to have the work done. Can the contractor impose a mechanic's lien on the homeowner's property under Connecticut law?

    1. No, in Connecticut a mechanic's lien attaches on the date the contract is signed or the work is ordered, and neither event occurred here.
    2. No, the homeowner cannot be forced to pay for the contractor's mistake.
    3. Yes, where a landowner knows of work being done on his or her property and does not object or disclaim responsibility, a mechanic's lien may be created.
    4. Yes, the homeowner should have mailed a notice of nonresponsibility to the contractor's main place of business.

133. To claim a mechanic's lien for materials supplied, a supplier must file a notice of the lien in the public record within

    1. 90 days after the material is supplied.
    2. six months after the material is supplied.
    3. 60 days after the material is supplied.
    4. 90 days after the work is started.

134. The usual test applied to the priority of liens (other than tax and municipal liens) is the date of

    1. recording.
    2. court filing.
    3. execution.
    4. the document.

135. In Connecticut, an individual may enter into legally enforceable contracts (with no exceptions) when he or she reaches the age of

    1. 16.
    2. 18.
    3. 19.
    4. 21.

136. In Connecticut, the prescriptive period to acquire an easement is

    1. 100 months.
    2. 12 years.
    3. 15 years.
    4. 30 years.

137. To be extinguished by law, a right-of-way must have been abandoned for at least

    1. 100 months.
    2. 12 years.
    3. 15 years.
    4. 30 years.

138. A neighbor has been crossing W's property to get to a state beach. W wishes to prevent the neighbor from acquiring an easement to cross his land. To do so effectively, W must

    1. follow Connecticut statutory procedures.
    2. write the neighbor a letter granting her permission to cross the property.
    3. write her a letter forbidding her to cross the property.
    4. put up a "No Trespassing" sign.

139. The prescriptive period in the state of Connecticut to acquire title to real property by adverse possession is

    1. 7 years.
    2. 10 years.
    3. 15 years.
    4. 20 years.

140. To acquire land by adverse possession requires use of the land

    1. with the owner's permission.
    2. for a period of 30 years.
    3. privately so as to avoid being seen.
    4. without the owner's permission.

141. Which of the following is an example of a license, and therefore not entitled to a claim of adverse possession?

1. A person who has been in possession of the property for 19 years
2. A person who held the property for five years after "inheriting" it from a parent, who was in adverse possession for 10 years
3. A person who has been entering an orchard and taking apples every October since 1972
4. A person who has been parking his or her car on a neighbor's property for 20 years without permission

142. A neighbor has a ten-foot easement through W's forested lot for the purpose of walking to the bank of the river. The neighbor widens the path to 14 feet to accommodate his truck so he can launch his boat. W is furious. Which of the following is true in this situation?

1. The neighbor's original use was a right; W can do nothing.
2. The new use is hostile and, if not stopped within 15 years, could become an easement by prescription.
3. The additional four feet is a reasonable extension of the original easement and must be granted.
4. If the neighbor uses the extension for 15 years, the original easement is his by adverse possession.

143. With respect to leases for terms in excess of one year, the landlord may record, instead of the actual lease, a

1. lis pendens.
2. rent supplement notice.
3. notice of constructive occupancy.
4. notice of lease.

144. A couple has signed a lease containing a provision to waive their rights to the interest earned from the security deposit. This provision is

1. unenforceable, thus making the lease invalid.
2. unenforceable, but the lease is still valid.
3. enforceable because all parties agreed to it.
4. enforceable only for the term of the lease.

145. When should a landlord first present the rules and regulations for tenants of leased property?

1. When the tenant first violates them
2. When the tenant requests them
3. At any time during the rental agreement
4. At the time the tenant enters into the rental agreement or at the time the rules or regulations are adopted

146. In Connecticut, a landlord may terminate the rental agreement if a tenant fails to pay rent within how many days of the scheduled due date?

1. 7 days
2. 9 days
3. 10 days
4. 30 days

147. Raising rents would not be deemed retaliatory if done to reflect a substantial increase in property taxes after

1. all other leases in the complex expire.
2. four months.
3. six months.
4. It is illegal to raise rents.

148. A tenant leased space in a warehouse and put down a two-month security deposit. What percent interest does her security deposit earn as long as she does not pay her rent late?

   1. 2 percent
   2. 4 percent
   3. 5 1/4 percent
   4. A rate tied to the average savings deposit rate

149. In Connecticut, if a monthly rental payment is made more than ten days after the due date, how much must the tenant forfeit on his or her security deposit?

   1. No interest
   2. One month's interest
   3. Two month's interest
   4. The whole year's interest

150. A tenant skips out on his last scheduled monthly payment on a one-year lease. The landlord may

   1. keep the tenant's belongings.
   2. sue the tenant for one month's rent.
   3. do nothing because the lease is terminated.
   4. extend the lease automatically because the tenant gave no notice.

151. If an evicted tenant does not remove his or her belongings, under summary process, the belongings of the evicted tenant may be

   1. used by the landlord.
   2. sold by the landlord.
   3. placed on the street by the sheriff.
   4. brought to the town dump.

152. If no one claims the proceeds of a sale resulting from the sale at public auction of the belongings of an evicted tenant within 30 days from such sale, these proceeds are turned over to the

   1. landlord, to offset the judgment.
   2. sheriff who executed the eviction.
   3. town treasury.
   4. state's general fund.

153. Assuming that there has been no damage to the property by the tenant, what must a landlord in Connecticut do with a tenant's security deposit at the end of a lease?

   1. The landlord is entitled to keep the security deposit.
   2. The landlord is only required to pay tenants' interest on the security deposits.
   3. The landlord cannot apply the security deposit to rent owed by the tenant.
   4. The landlord must return the security deposit to the tenant within 30 days of the end of the lease.

154. One landlord owns a three-unit apartment building. Another is the landlord of a 30-unit apartment building. Based on these facts, which of the following is true of security deposits under Connecticut law?

    1. Both landlords must give tenants an itemized statement of alleged damages before they can withhold any part of the security deposit as compensation.
    2. Only the landlord of the 30-unit building is required to pay interest on security deposits.
    3. Only the landlord of the three-unit is required to give tenants an itemized statement of alleged damages before any part of the security deposit may be withheld as compensation.
    4. Neither landlord is required to pay interest on security.

155. In order to enforce the provisions of a two-year lease, the lease would have to be

    1. either oral or in writing.
    2. in writing.
    3. recorded.
    4. written on a standard Connecticut lease form.

156. In Connecticut, if a landlord wants to terminate a periodic tenancy, how much notice must the tenant receive?

    1. 7 days
    2. One month
    3. 60 days
    4. One year

157. A landlord of a residential condominium charges $750 per month for an apartment. What is the maximum amount the landlord can require as a security deposit?

    1. $750
    2. $1,000
    3. $1,500
    4. $2,250

158. After the lease terminates, a tenant is entitled to the return of his or her security deposit

    1. within 30 days, including interest.
    2. within three weeks, including interest.
    3. unless the property has been transferred to a new owner.
    4. with no deduction withheld.

159. A tenant's lease runs from September 1 to August 31, with rent payable the first of every month. At the end of May, the tenant vacates the property and does not make the last three rent payments. Given that there is a great demand for rental housing, the landlord is able to re-rent the apartment at the beginning of July for the same rent. The landlord can sue the original tenant for

    1. three months' rent.
    2. two months' rent.
    3. one month's rent.
    4. nothing.

160. After a heated argument about rent increases, a tenant spray paints the kitchen black and smashes the sink to bits, causing approximately $2,300 in damage. The tenant may

   1. be arrested.
   2. lose his or her entire security deposit of $3,000.
   3. be subject to an additional rent increase to cover the damage.
   4. abandon the property because it is no longer fit for living.

161. How soon must deeds of conveyance be recorded after closing?

   1. A reasonable time
   2. One business day
   3. Three business days
   4. One month

162. In Connecticut, the local official who records deeds and maintains the grantor/grantee lists is the

   1. first selectman.
   2. assessor.
   3. tax collector.
   4. town clerk.

163. A woman buys her home with her fiancée prior to marriage. After her marriage she changes her name. This name change must be given to the town clerk in the town where their home is located within

   1. 30 days.
   2. 60 days.
   3. 90 days.
   4. one year.

164. A homeowner's property is being foreclosed on through a strict foreclosure process. The homeowner has the right to redeem the property

   1. on the law day provided by the court.
   2. by being the successful bidder at the foreclosure sale.
   3. by redeeming the property within one year of title's passing to the foreclosing creditor.
   4. by matching the successful bidder's bid within one year of the foreclosure sale.

165. In Connecticut, if an owner defaults on his or her mortgage loan and the property is ordered sold at a foreclosure sale, the owner may redeem the property

   1. prior to the sale, under the statutory right of redemption.
   2. prior to the sale, under the equitable right of redemption.
   3. at the sale, bidding successfully on the property.
   4. after the sale, under the statutory right of equity of redemption.

166. How long is the defaulted borrower's redemption period after a foreclosure sale is complete?

   1. One year
   2. Six months
   3. Three years
   4. There is no redemption period.

167. The Connecticut statutes require a complete revaluation of real properties in any given town once every

    1. year.
    2. five years.
    3. twelve years.
    4. time the grand list increases by ten percent.

168. In Connecticut, real property taxes are based on the owner's

    1. assessment ratio.
    2. income.
    3. property values.
    4. ability to pay.

169. In Connecticut, real property taxes are payable on

    1. July 1.
    2. July 1 and January 1.
    3. January 1.
    4. June 30 and December 31.

170. From a strictly legal standpoint, real property taxes become a lien on the property as of the

    1. due date.
    2. thirtieth day from the due date.
    3. date of assessment.
    4. date a foreclosure suit is filed and recorded.

171. The conveyance tax levied by the state on the seller of the property is based on

    1. the selling price.
    2. earnest money.
    3. the amount of the mortgage.
    4. the date of the purchase.

172. For property tax purposes in Connecticut, none of the following lands would be assessed at market value EXCEPT

    1. farm land.
    2. forest land.
    3. contaminated land.
    4. open space land.

173. A property owner who feels that his or her property has been assessed incorrectly may appeal to the

    1. local board of tax review.
    2. state board of tax review.
    3. tax commissioner's office.
    4. tax assessor's office.

174. A recently recorded deed states that the purchase price was "$10 and other good and valuable consideration." The conveyance tax stamp indicates that $192.50 was paid for town conveyance tax. What was the property sold for?

    1. $10
    2. $21,175
    3. $175,000
    4. $192,500

175. The state wishes to widen a highway. It exercises its right of eminent domain and takes a portion of a property through condemnation proceedings. The conveyance tax on this conveyance to the state would be

    1. one-half the usual.
    2. zero.
    3. the same as usual but picked up by the state.
    4. $250, regardless of the consideration amount.

176. What is the total conveyance tax on a property that sells for $250,000?

    1. $275
    2. $550
    3. $1,250
    4. $1,525

177. What is the town conveyance tax on a property that sells for $185,000?

    1. $18.50
    2. $92.50
    3. $203.50
    4. $1,850

178. A house was sold for $150,000, with the buyers assuming a $40,000 mortgage. How much will the total conveyance tax be?

    1. $915
    2. $750
    3. $671
    4. $550

179. If an aggrieved person is awarded a judgment against a real estate licensee for violation of the Connecticut licensing laws, which of the following correctly states the aggrieved party's rights regarding the guaranty fund?

    1. He or she has the right, under the license law, to immediately recover the full judgment amount plus court costs and attorney's fees from the guaranty fund.
    2. He or she has the right to a maximum award amount of $25,000 from the guaranty fund, including court costs and attorney's fees.
    3. He or she has the right to sue the Connecticut Real Estate Commission for misdeeds in state superior court.
    4. He or she has the right to a $10,000 maximum recovery from the guaranty fund, plus limited court costs and attorney's fees.

180. The purpose of the Connecticut Real Estate Guaranty Fund is to

1. ensure that Connecticut real estate licensees have adequate funds available to pay their licensing and continuing education fees.
2. provide a means of compensation for actual monetary losses suffered by individuals as a result of the acts of a licensee who has violated the license law or committed other illegal acts related to a real estate transaction.
3. protect the real estate commission from claims by individuals that they have suffered a monetary loss as the result of the action of a licensee who has violated the license law or committed other illegal acts related to a real estate transaction.
4. provide an interest-generating source of revenue to fund the activities of the real estate commission.

181. Who may receive compensation from the real estate guaranty fund?

1. Broker who does not receive an earned commission
2. Seller who pays a commission to a broker under false pretenses
3. Buyer who pays a fee to a broker under a buyer agency agreement
4. Cooperating broker who does not receive a commission split

182. The maximum compensation that will be paid from the real estate guaranty fund for any single transaction is

1. $5,000.
2. $10,000.
3. $25,000.
4. $55,000.

183. Whenever the commission is required to satisfy a claim against a licensee with money from the real estate guaranty fund, the

1. licensee may continue engaging in real estate activities under the commission's direct supervision.
2. licensee must repay the full amount plus interest to the account if his or her license is to be reinstated.
3. aggrieved party may later collect additional damages by forcing the sale of any property newly acquired by the defendant licensee.
4. licensee must thereafter pay $25 per year into the account when applying to renew his or her license.

184. What is the maximum balance of the Connecticut Real Estate Guaranty Fund?

1. $400,000
2. $500,000
3. $750,000
4. There is no maximum.

185. After proper investigation, a payment is made from the Connecticut Real Estate Guaranty Fund due to the improper activities of a licensee. What happens when the payment is made?

1. The licensee's license is automatically suspended.
2. The commission takes no further action if the licensee repays the fund within 30 days.
3. The licensee's license is automatically revoked.
4. The licensee is subject to a fine of $2,000.

186. A broker commits a fraudulent act in connection with the sale of a property on March 15, 1999. On March 30, the transaction closes. On November 1, the client sues the broker, alleging fraud. On December 20, the jury finds in favor of the client. The client must file a claim with the real estate commission to recover money from the guaranty fund within

    1. 30 days following the illegal activity, in this case, by April 15, 1999.
    2. 2 years after having been awarded a judgment by the courts, in this case, by December 20, 2001.
    3. 1 year of filing suit, in this case, by November 1, 2000.
    4. 2 years of the date of closing; in this case, by March 30, 2001.

187. In Connecticut, dower and curtesy are

    1. currently recognized.
    2. recognized voluntarily.
    3. recognized but not enforced.
    4. not recognized.

188. A man and woman are married and live in a home owned by the wife. If the wife dies, the husband

    1. will be entitled to a one-third life estate in the home.
    2. will be entitled to a life estate in the home.
    3. comes into a life estate because of a homestead right.
    4. comes into a life estate because of a curtesy right.

189. What is the status of dower and curtesy rights in Connecticut?

    1. Dower and curtesy have been abolished.
    2. Dower is a fee simple estate; curtesy is a life estate.
    3. Dower and curtesy are identical rights in fee simple estate.
    4. Dower and curtesy have been combined by statute into one right.

190. All of the following forms of ownership are recognized under Connecticut law EXCEPT

    1. tenancy in common.
    2. joint tenancy with survivorship rights.
    3. condominium ownership.
    4. tenancy by the entirety.

191. A husband and wife, who own their home as joint tenants, obtain a divorce. At that time, the joint tenancy

    1. extinguishes and becomes a tenancy in common.
    2. continues until one of them dies.
    3. extinguishes and becomes a tenancy at sufferance.
    4. reverts to common interest ownership.

192. To establish a "marketable record title," an unbroken chain of title must be established for a period of at least

    1. 15 years.
    2. 20 years.
    3. 40 years.
    4. 60 years.

193. Unless stated to the contrary in a deed, ownership of land by a married couple is assumed to be by

1. severalty.
2. joint tenancy.
3. tenancy in common.
4. tenancy by the entirety.

194. A buyer enters into a purchase and sale contract to buy a house on October 15. The closing occurs on November 15, at which time the seller delivers the deed. The deed is recorded on November 17. The buyer moves into the property on November 18. In Connecticut, title would have passed from the seller to the buyer on

1. October 15.
2. November 15.
3. November 17.
4. November 18.

195. A husband owns a rental property occupied by a tenant. The wife has no ownership interest in the property. If the husband wants to sell the property, who is required by law to sign the listing agreement?

1. Both the husband and the wife because they are a married couple
2. The husband only
3. The husband as owner and the tenant in possession
4. The husband, wife, and tenant

196. A property owner purchased his house twelve years ago, and is now interested in selling it. Unfortunately, he has either lost or misplaced his original deed. A copy of the recorded deed from the town clerk's office will

1. be useless.
2. indicate only equitable title.
3. serve as prima facie evidence of title.
4. need to be notarized by the original closing attorney.

197. When searching title in Connecticut, documents affecting title can be found in the

1. county land records office.
2. state land records office.
3. town land records office.
4. town abstractor's office.

198. The grantor list in a town contains

1. information on local real estate transactions indexed under the name of the grantor.
2. information on local real estate transactions indexed under the name of the grantee.
3. original copies of all local real estate transaction deeds signed by grantors.
4. information on real property donated to the town and other large grants and gifts.

199. If a body of water adjoining an upland property owner's property is navigable, the property owner's boundary is the

1. mean high tide line (water's edge).
2. center of the body of water.
3. mean low tide line.
4. base line meridian.

200. A nonnavigable stream runs through a property owner's land. The property owner can do all of the following EXCEPT

1. own the underlying stream bed.
2. use the water as a source of power.
3. dam up the stream to create a small pond.
4. use the stream as a source of drinking water.

201. The Connecticut Real Estate Commission has the authority to

1. apply and enforce the rules by which all real estate licensees must abide.
2. compose the examination questions on the state exam.
3. administer the exams given at the testing sites.
4. enact the laws that govern real estate licensees.

202. In Connecticut, the basic unit of real property tax rate is called a(n)

1. assessment ratio.
2. quota.
3. mill rate.
4. equalization factor.

Answer Key

1. (1) The broker earned the commission since the seller formally accepted the offer. The fact that a sale may not actually take place or that a seller defaults on a contract does not change the right of a licensed broker to recover a commission. Further, the deposit must be returned to the buyer, and the broker cannot take his or her commission from it.

2. (4) Yes, if the buyer and seller both give their informed consent to dual agency Connecticut permits dual agency if both parties (seller/buyer or landlord/tenant) give their informed consent to the dual agency. Payment of commission does not dictate agency relationships.

3. (2) Confidential information must remain confidential even after the termination of an agency agreement. The original listing agent is not a dual agent, since the original agent no longer has an agency relationship with the seller; the original listing agent is now free to represent the buyer. Agents must always disclose information about the physical condition of the property.

4. (1) In Connecticut, a real estate licensee may not receive any type of referral fee for the referral of any buyer to a mortgage lender or broker. Furthermore, salespeople can only receive compensation from their employing brokers.

5. (3) A licensee that has not entered into an agency relationship with a buyer is precluded from asking the buyer to disclose confidential information. To prequalify the buyer, the salesperson would need to ask the buyer about the buyer's financial status, which is confidential. The agent can provide the buyer with information on properties for sale in the area, give information on mortgage interest rates and terms, and explain agency to the buyer.

6. (3) In Connecticut, a licensee can work with a buyer as a customer. In this instance, the licensee would represent the seller; therefore, in order to work with the buyer, the licensee would need to provide the buyer with an agency disclosure notice stating that the licensee represents the seller, not the buyer. Working with a buyer in a nonagency context, while representing the seller in an agency context, does not constitute dual agency. The salesperson would not need to obtain the seller's permission since there is no dual agency and no subagency.

7. (3) Buyers can enter into an exclusive-right-to-buy agreement, but this type of relationship must be clearly identified in the agreement.

8. (1) The buyer-brokerage contract is an employment contract and must be in writing to be enforceable. These contracts are regulated under license laws and are legal.

9.　(2) The Connecticut Real Estate Commission's rules regarding listing agreements do not include the requirement that they be accompanied by a qualified expert's report of the property's condition. The licensing law requires that listing agreements identify the compensation to be paid to the broker, be in writing and signed by both broker and seller, and contain a statement regarding brokers' lien rights.

10.　(3) Connecticut does not recognize transaction agency. Connecticut allows dual agency (with the informed consent of both parties), buyer's agency, and subagency (with the consent of the seller).

11.　(3) Dual compensation is allowed in dual agency as long as both parties give their informed consent to the dual compensation arrangement.

12.　(1) A firm working with a buyer who has not entered into a buyer agency agreement is allowed to show houses listed with another firm only if the seller (not the seller's brokerage firm) of the house gives consent to the subagency relationship.

13.　(3) Seller property disclosure reports are required in the transfer of one- to four-dwelling residential units, whether or not the seller is represented by a broker or has resided on the property. The sale of commercial property does not require this property condition disclosure report.

14.　(1) The seller must deliver the property condition disclosure report to a prospective purchaser prior to a written offer.

15.　(2) The disclosures are required to be based on the seller's actual knowledge of the condition of the property. Since the seller has no knowledge of any plumbing system problems on the property, she should respond "no."

16.　(4) Connecticut statute requires property disclosures be made for the sale of all one to four dwelling units. The agent should encourage the seller to be honest and disclose known problems.

17.　(2) In Connecticut, a salesperson may work with a prospective buyer as a customer while representing the seller. In this instance, the salesperson would provide the buyer with a written agency disclosure notice stating that the salesperson represents the seller at the first personal meeting with the buyer at which the buyer's needs are discussed. This notice must be made so that the buyer understands that he or she is not being represented.

18.　(3) Licensees and owners are not liable to buyers for failure to disclose that a property was occupied by a person who was HIV-positive or had AIDS or that a suicide, murder, or other felony occurred on the property unless the buyer advises the licensee or seller in writing that information that may have a psychological impact is important for his or her decision.

19. (4) The salesperson will have to inform the owner in writing that the salesperson is a licensee before making the offer. The salesperson does not have to resign, should not use a third party, and would not need to get the commission involved.

20. (1) The buyer can sue the broker for nondisclosure since it is a violation of license law. Connecticut licensing laws specifically prohibit a licensee from concealing any material fact in a transaction. The fact that the buyer did not ask is not relevant. Further, the seller may also be liable for nondisclosure under common law theories of nondisclosure.

21. (4) A licensee representing the seller is only required to give the agency disclosure notice to an unrepresented prospective buyer.

22. (3) The licensee owes a duty of confidentiality to the tenant who hired the licensee. The disclosure was a violation of this fiduciary duty and the licensing laws. Further, representation is determined by who does the hiring, not who pays the fee.

23. (4) A sale by a real estate licensee of a two-unit apartment building requires a property condition disclosure report. A foreclosure sale, gift, and conveyance from one spouse to another are specifically exempted from the disclosure requirement by statute.

24. (1) The buyer does not know what her relationship or the seller's relationship is to the salesperson. Agency representation is not about the property, rather, the duties and obligations to a client and a customer. In this instance, a salesperson is required to give an unrepresented prospective buyer an agency disclosure notice at the first personal meeting with the buyer where the buyer's needs are discussed.

25. (3) The broker must disclose the cracked foundation, but not the suicide. Discussing the suicide could constitute a breach of duty to the client. Licensees and owners are not liable to buyers for failure to disclose that a property was occupied by a person who was HIV-positive or had AIDS, or that a suicide, murder, or other felony occurred on the property unless the purchaser advises the licensee or owner in writing that information that may have a psychological impact is important for his or her decision.

26. (2) Buyer agency is allowed in Connecticut. In a cooperating sale scenario, typically the cooperating broker represents the buyer, otherwise the cooperating broker would need to get the seller's consent to subagency. A broker must represent only one party in a transaction. Connecticut does not recognize nonagency.

27. (4) A broker representing the seller is required to give an agency disclosure notice only to an unrepresented buyer; timing of the disclosure must be at the first personal meeting where the prospective buyer's needs are discussed.

28. (1) A dual agent may provide comparable market data to the seller; and if such information is requested by one party, it must be provided to both. Connecticut law specifically provides that certain information cannot be disclosed in a dual agency situation, including the disclosure of the buyer's financial qualifications to the seller, telling the buyer that the seller will accept less than the listing price, or that the buyer will pay more than the offering price.

29. (4) Subagency is restricted in Connecticut. While Connecticut law permits subagency, it can only be entered into with the specific consent of the seller. A broker's blanket offer of subagency through MLS is not permitted.

30. (3) This is a dual agency situation because it is an in-house transaction. Dual agency is permitted in Connecticut if both the buyer and seller give their informed consent to the dual agency. The listing and selling salespeople do not need to be separate individuals for dual agency to be allowed.

31. (4) Connecticut allows designated agency. When a brokerage firm represents both the buyer and the seller (dual agency), the broker may designate one salesperson to represent the buyer and another to represent the seller (designated agency). The salespeople would not be dual agents, although the brokerage firm, broker, and other salespeople in the firm would be considered dual agents.

32. (1) Connecticut allows for a broker who has performed services relating to residential or commercial real estate to place a lien on the real estate to secure payment of compensation. The claim of the lien must be recorded prior to conveyance.

33. (4) Real estate commissions are always negotiable between the seller/buyer and broker.

34. (2) In order to enter into a client relationship with a buyer or seller, Connecticut requires that the buyer/seller and broker enter into a written agency agreement. The broker has only entered into a written agreement with the seller, therefore, the seller is the broker's client. The broker is allowed to work with the prospective buyer without having entered into a written agreement; in this case, the prospective buyer is the broker's customer, not client, and there is no agency relationship between them.

35. (4) The broker cannot withhold a material fact from a potential purchaser. The fact that the basement floods is a material fact. The agent should explain to the seller that he must disclose this material fact. Such disclosure does not violate the agent's fiduciary duty to his or her client.

36. (1) Such disclosures violate the broker's fiduciary duty to his or her client. The broker is only required to disclose material facts about the physical condition of the property, not about his or her client's personal situation.

37. (4) Connecticut allows licensees to work with buyers in a customer, rather than client, capacity. This would be the case here, if the prospective buyer and the broker do not enter into a written buyer agency agreement.

38. (3) Connecticut's agency disclosure notice is given to an unrepresented party in a transaction, at the time the licensee first personally meets with the unrepresented person to discuss his or her needs. Here, the prospective buyer is unrepresented, and would be given the agency disclosure notice.

39. (3) There are three basic types of buyer agency agreements, similar to the three types of listing agreements. With an exclusive buyer agency agreement, the broker is paid a commission if the client buys a property, regardless of whether the broker introduced the property to the client.

40. (4) Connecticut allows dual agency if both buyer and seller give their informed consent to it.

41. (3) Connecticut allows for a designated option to dual agency. With designated agency, a firm can designate one salesperson to represent the buyer and another to represent the seller, in which case neither salesperson would be a dual agent. The firm's managing broker and other nondesignated salespeople would still be dual agents, and the parties would have to give their consent.

42. (2) The Connecticut Real Estate Commission administers the real estate licensing laws. The Connecticut Commission on Human Rights and Opportunities handles fair housing complaints. The Connecticut Association of REALTORS® is a trade association. The Department of Housing and Urban Development is a federal government agency supervising housing issues.

43. (1) In Connecticut, the governor makes appointments to the real estate commission.

44. (1) A leasing agent would need to be licensed, with the exception of resident apartment managers who are specifically exempted from licensing requirements. Attorneys serving as legal counsel for clients are not required to be licensed, nor are partners selling their own property required to have a real estate license.

45. (2) Matching individuals for a fee or commission requires a real estate license. Resident managers, nonprofits, and court-appointed persons are specifically exempt.

46. (1) Under Connecticut law, any person who acts as a real property securities dealer must hold a Connecticut real estate license.

47. (1) The designated broker of a partnership, association or corporation must hold a broker's license. Employees are not required to hold broker's licenses, although employees who are independent contractors actively participating in the real estate business must hold either a broker's or salesperson's license. Filing papers with the secretary of state is a requirement for incorporation, not for real estate licensing. Licensees, not a firm, must pay a one-time fee to the guaranty fund.

48. (1) Managing real estate is not included in the definition of real estate activities requiring a license, while reselling a mobile home, selling real estate, and renting real estate on behalf of a resident landlord are included in licensing requirements.

49. (1) Attorneys at law when serving as legal counsel to their client are specifically exempt from the licensing requirement. If engaging in real estate activities, appraisers, associations, partnerships, corporations, and real property security dealers must have a real estate license.

50. (4) The office manager is performing non-real estate activities and is therefore exempt from licensing requirements.

51. (1) Applications must be completed before taking the written exam. The commission does not require a photo. Testing is done on an on-going basis throughout the year. Applicants do not have to supply sworn statements attesting to their character in order to take the test.

52. (3) An applicant for a broker's license must be actively engaged in real estate for only two years, not three. Applicants must have completed 90 hours of approved real estate courses, be at least 18 years of age, and submit letters of character reference.

53. (4) State law prohibits lawsuits to collect commissions unless the injured party is a licensed broker and the license was in effect at the time the real estate services were rendered.

54. (4) An applicant for a real estate license in Connecticut must show proof of passing the license examination. No college is required as a prerequisite to real estate licensing. A person must be 18 years of age to apply for a real estate license. Connecticut will not automatically refuse to issue a license to an applicant who has been convicted of a felony.

55. (2) The commission can impose as a penalty a fine not to exceed $1,000 and/or up to a six-month prison term.

56. (3) Licenses expire May 31 annually, although continuing education requirements must be met by May 31 of every even-numbered year.

57. (4) To renew a salesperson's license, every year a salesperson must pay a fee of $225. In addition, in even-numbered years, a salesperson must show proof of having completed 12 hours of CE credit.

58. (4) Licenses are renewed annually May 31.

59. (2) Salespersons must take 12 hours of CE every two years, including three hours of a law/fair housing update.

60. (3) Explaining simple contract documents to prospective buyers is a real estate service that may only be performed by a licensee. Computing commission checks is a bookkeeping act may be performed under the direction of a licensee. Assembling legal documents required for a closing is a secretarial act and may be performed under the direction of a licensee. Preparing and distributing flyers and promotional materials is an advertising act and may be performed under the direction of a licensee.

61. (2) Some assistants are unlicensed, performing only ministerial duties. Typing contract forms under the employing broker's supervision and approval is secretarial in nature and does not require licensing. Personal assistants may be licensed in order to perform more services for the licensee who hired them and only these licensed personal assistants may independently host open houses.

62. (3) Unlicensed assistants are not permitted to perform the described services. Both the broker and the personal assistant are in violation of rules regarding unlicensed assistants.

63. (4) All nonresident applicants must file an irrevocable consent to suit with the Connecticut Real Estate Commission, which enables suits and actions to be brought against the nonresident licensee in Connecticut as though he or she were a resident licensee. The Commission may grant a license to a licensed broker or salesperson from another state that has substantially similar licensing requirements and grants reciprocity to Connecticut real estate licensees. A person obtaining a reciprocal license is not required to take the Connecticut education courses, the Connecticut exam, or establish a place of business in Connecticut.

64. (2) All nonresident applicants must file an irrevocable consent to suit with the commission, which enables suits and actions to be brought against the nonresident licensee in Connecticut as though he or she were a resident licensee.

65. (1) Any individual may sell his or her own house, without hiring a licensee or attorney, and without obtaining a license.

66. (4) The education requirement for a salesperson's license is 30 hours of an approved principles and practices course. There is no citizenship or degree requirement for a license. After obtaining a license, a salesperson would need to take 12 hours of continuing education credit every two years, three hours of which would be in law/fair housing.

67. (4) In Connecticut, all real estate licenses expire annually on May 31.

68. (3) A real estate license is required for anyone engaging in the real estate business, which includes listing real estate for sale, selling, buying, renting, exchanging real estate, or collecting rent for the use of real estate, and reselling a mobile home for another and for a fee. Constructing houses does not require a real estate license, nor are licenses required of individuals who are buying or selling a house for themselves.

69. (4) The real estate commission maintains a guaranty fund to compensate persons who are aggrieved by a licensee through embezzlement, false pretenses, trickery, fraud, or misrepresentation. It is not meant to compensate licensees, but persons working with licensees.

70. (2) A licensee is allowed to be a dual agent, as long as all parties give their informed consent to dual agency. The licensing laws specifically list grounds for revocation of a real estate license, which include misrepresenting the size of the property, including automatic extensions in listings, and working for more than one broker.

71. (4) The correct venue for appealing a commission license revocation is either to the Hartford-New Britain Superior Court or the superior court for the judicial district in which the licensee resides.

72. (4) Commission rates are always negotiable between the seller and the broker. Section 20-320 of the Connecticut licensing laws gives the commission the power to temporarily suspend or permanently revoke a license if it finds the licensee guilty of a number of prohibited activities, including commingling of funds, failing to provide signed copies of documents, and being convicted of a felony.

73. (4) Section 20-320 of the Connecticut licensing laws gives the commission the power to temporarily suspend or permanently revoke a license if it finds the licensee guilty of a number of prohibited activities, including commingling of personal and client funds. Depositing a buyer's down payment in a personal bank account would constitute commingling. A salesperson may represent only one broker at a time, unless the salesperson has his or her broker's consent. Buyer representation and exclusive-listing contracts are permitted.

74. (2) Depositing an earnest money deposit in a firm's escrow account is proper conduct. Section 20-320 of the Connecticut licensing laws gives the Commission the power to temporarily suspend or permanently revoke a license if it finds the licensee guilty of a number of prohibited activities, including fraud. Cheating on the licensing exam would constitute fraud, and therefore is grounds for revocation. Additionally, the Commission can revoke a license if the licensee violates any provisions of the licensing laws. Giving an agency disclosure notice to an unrepresented party is required by the licensing laws; therefore failing to abide by this requirement is grounds for license revocation. Displaying a sign on a property without the owner's consent is in violation of the licensing laws, and therefore grounds for revocation.

75. (3) Connecticut licensing law specifically prohibits a licensee from misrepresenting the selling price to any lender or any other interested party. Such action would constitute fraud and dishonest dealings, for which the commission has the power to revoke a licensee's license.

76. (4) All advertisements must include the name of the employing broker, but do not need to state a license number, the expiration date of the license, or the street address.

77. (1) Connecticut licensing laws specifically prohibit a licensee from placing a sign on a property without the consent of the owner of the property or his or her duly authorized agent or fiduciary. The licensee does not have to obtain the consent of the neighbors.

78. (3) All advertising must be made in the name of the employing broker. There is no requirement that advertisements contain the name of the owner, street address, box number, or even a telephone number to call.

79. (3) When acting as a private citizen, the salesperson need not disclose license status in advertising but will have to disclose this fact before an offer is accepted.

80. (3) Net listings are illegal at any time because of potential conflict of interest for the broker.

81. (3) Net listings are illegal in Connecticut. This is a good example of the conflict of interest that a net listing provokes as the broker was not working in the best interest of his client.

82. (4) Commissions are always negotiable between the principal and the agent. Commission rates are not determined by a local groups of brokers, nor by law, nor by the real estate commission.

83. (1) Commissions are always negotiable between the principal and the agent and are not determined by custom or law. The commission may be not be deducted from the earnest money deposit. Commissions may not be shared with an unlicensed party.

84. (2) Any funds accepted by a broker must be deposited within three banking days from the date the agreement evidencing such transaction is signed by all the necessary parties.

85. (1) Connecticut has a special program for use of interest earned on real estate broker escrow and trust accounts. Deposits that are less than $10,000 and held for not more than 60 days, are to be deposited into an interest-bearing account where the interest is directed to be paid to the Connecticut Housing Authority. All brokers are required to participate. A client, however, may request that his or her deposit not be part of this program, in which case the deposit is to be put in a separate interest-bearing account.

86. (4) The broker should have deposited the money in a special bank account, and should have discussed the interest with the parties. Connecticut has a special program for use of interest earned on real estate broker escrow and trust accounts. Deposits that are less than $10,000 and are held for not more than 60 days are to be deposited in an interest-bearing account where the interest is directed to be paid to the Connecticut Housing Authority. All brokers are required to participate. A client, however, may request that his or her deposit not be part of this program, in which case the deposit is to be put in a separate interest-bearing account.

87. (2) Proper identification of the property, such as the property address, is required, but not the legal description. A written listing agreement must state that the broker's compensation is not fixed by law and is negotiable, the expiration date, and a statement acknowledging adherence to the Connecticut statutes pertaining to fair housing.

88. (2) Listings must contain a definite termination date and rollover extensions are not permitted under Connecticut law.

89. (2) Lack of a specific termination date is grounds for suspension or revocation of a real estate license.

90. (4) The listing broker must give the seller an executed copy. Numbering files, advertising, and cooperating with other brokers are not required.

91. (2) The listing agreement may be canceled but the seller may be responsible for some expenses. The Connecticut Real Estate Commission will not be involved.

92. (4) Fair housing complaints are generally directed to HUD or the Human Rights Commission. REALTOR® organizations do not receive discrimination complaints.

93. (2) A complaint must be filed with the Connecticut Commission on Human Rights and Opportunities within 180 days after the alleged act of discrimination.

94. (4) The landlord of residential property must allow a tenant to modify a unit to make it accessible if the tenant is willing to pay to have it done.

95. (2) Salespeople should be careful to avoid the unlawful practice of law by writing such a clause. Only a licensed attorney may legitimately prepare this clause for inclusion in the sales contract.

96. (2) Salespeople may collect compensation only from their employing brokers.

97. (3) In Connecticut, the salesperson is responsible for notifying the commission about a change of brokerage affiliation. There is a $25 transfer fee that must be paid along with this notification.

98. (1) A salesperson may be licensed with only one broker. A salesperson may represent another broker, after obtaining consent from his or her affiliated broker, but this does not mean that the salesperson would also hold his or her license with the other broker.

99. (4) Accepting the money is a violation of commission regulations. A salesperson or associate broker may collect a fee only from his or her employing broker.

100. (4) The broker can say "thank you" to the pilot. A broker may pay a referral fee only to someone who holds a real estate license.

101. (4) One example of a fee request that is not considered a "reasonable cause for payment" is when a relocation company policy requires such a fee in order to work with a broker. The commission's policy guidance on what constitutes a reasonable cause for payment includes the following: an actual introduction of business has been made, a subagency relationship exists or a contractual referral fee relationship exists.

102. (2) The clerk of the court in which the conviction takes place is required by law to forward a certified copy of the conviction to the commission.

103. (1) Under Connecticut's Common Interest Ownership Act, resale purchasers of condominiums have the right to cancel the contract within five business days after a resale certificate has been delivered to them.

104. (1) Commissions are always negotiable between the broker and the seller. The commission does not set commission rates. Local and state associations do not set commissions; if they did they would most likely be in violation of antitrust laws.

105. (3) Connecticut licensing laws require that a broker immediately provide a copy of any instrument to any party executing it. Other people's money must not be placed in a personal bank account. Completing a false, second purchase agreement for the purposes of obtaining a larger loan is prohibited under any circumstances. All written offers must be presented to the seller immediately.

106. (1) In Connecticut, the age of legal competence is 18.

107. (4) A person's amount of income is not a protected class under the Connecticut fair housing law. Although "lawful source of income" is a protected class (defined as income derived from Social Security, supplemental security income, housing assistance, child support, alimony, or public or general assistance), that is different from a straightforward amount. Protected classes in Connecticut include familial status, disability, and sexual preference.

108. (4) Mortgage loans for more than $5,000 are automatically exempted from usury regulations. Thus there is no ceiling on the interest rates that may be charged on real estate loans in Connecticut.

109. (4) In the event that no legal heirs or assigns can be identified within 20 years of a decedent's demise, the estate of that individual passes to the state by escheat.

110. (2) In Connecticut, defective lead-based paint must be abated if a child under the age of six lives in the residence. If a child has an elevated blood lead level, some intact surfaces may also need to be abated.

111. (3) The owner should disclose the presence of the tank to a potential purchaser because (1) if the owner does not, the purchaser can rescind the transaction, and (2) it is a material fact and concealing it would constitute fraud. Property owners in Connecticut can be held liable for cleanup costs and damage associated with leaking underground storage tanks, and sellers who do not disclose the presence of an underground tank to a buyer may have to take the property back. Further, many municipalities in Connecticut have enacted ordinances requiring the removal of older residential underground storage tanks.

112. (2) When an individual purchases property covered under Connecticut's Interstate Land Sales Act, he or she must be presented with a clearly identified copy of the prospectus, property report, or offering statement within 72 hours before signing a sales contract.

113. (1) Land court certificates are generally not utilized in Connecticut. A full abstract, certificate of title, and/or title search and opinion may be used.

114. (1) Should a foreclosure sale not produce enough funds to satisfy the foreclosing lender, the court may order a deficiency judgment against the borrower.

115. (1) The Connecticut Affordable Housing Land Use Appeals Act provides an affordable housing appeals procedure when a municipality denies a developer's affordable housing development. Its purpose is to encourage the development of affordable housing in the state, not mandate the construction of affordable housing, nor establish construction standards for affordable housing.

116. (2) The broker receives his or her commission check when the closing takes place and funds are disbursed, in this example, June 10.

117. (3) The closing attorney is responsible for calculating the prorations between the buyer and seller, searching the title, and preparing the mortgage note and deed.

118. (4) Conducting a title search may lead to charges of practicing law without a license. The broker could be responsible for the other activities: maintaining a time schedule and providing net data, explaining closing procedures to both the buyer and the seller and anticipate decision-making alternatives, and coordinating inspections and delivering documents.

119. (1) In Connecticut, it is customary for the seller to pay the property expenses for the day of closing.

120. (3) The wife receives all of the jointly held property and $125,000 of the separate property. Under Connecticut's Intestate Distribution Laws for separately held property, a decedent's spouse takes the first $100,000 plus half the remainder. The other half is divided evenly among the remaining children.

121. (1) The beneficiaries of a will may not sign as a witness unless they are also heirs of the testator. If a non-heir beneficiary signs as a witness, the will is not void, but the non-heir beneficiary runs the risk of being excluded from his or her devise.

122. (2) If a person designated to receive a share dies before a decedent's property is distributed, that person's descendants may receive it instead. Therefore, the daughter and remaining son each take $266,666, and the first son's children each take $133,333. An heir would not be denied because he or she was adopted.

123. (2) In Connecticut, a will may be prepared by anyone of sound mind who is at least 18 years of age.

124. (2) Two witnesses must sign in the presence of the person making the will.

125. (1) The interest of a person in the property of his or her spouse is provided for via statutory survivorship rights under the laws pertaining to the property rights of a husband or wife or, in the case of jointly held property, to joint tenancy with survivorship rights. Connecticut does not recognize dower or curtesy.

126. (3) Connecticut does recognize a homestead exemption in debt collection procedures for the purpose of protecting a person's equity in his or her home.

127. (2) A homeowner subject to a debt collection procedure may exempt his or her homestead from the collection up to a value of $75,000. Debts not included in this exemption are loans secured by a mortgage on the property, mechanics' liens, tax liens, and other liens consented by the homeowner. Therefore the creditors would receive $165,000 less $75,000, or $90,000.

128. (4) A homeowner subject to a debt collection procedure may exempt his or her homestead from the collection up to a value of $75,000. Debts not included in this exemption are loans secured by a mortgage on the property, mechanics' liens, tax liens, and other liens consented to by the homeowner.

129. (3) For legal descriptions of property, Connecticut predominantly follows the metes-and-bounds method.

130. (4) Monuments are used to establish boundaries; commonly these monuments are iron pins.

131. (1) The mechanic has 90 days to file the lien, which is effective as of the date construction was completed. Thus, the mechanic is first, then the mortgage companies as recorded.

132. (3) Under Connecticut law, the contractor may impose a mechanic's lien on the homeowner's property where a landowner knows of work being done on his or her property and does not object or disclaim responsibility.

133. (1) The mechanic may file a lien within 90 days of the supply of materials, or in the case of a contractor, 90 days from the time the mechanic's work ceases.

134. (1) Lien priority is based on the date of recording. Tax liens, however, take precedence.

135. (2) Legal age with no exceptions is 18. Some exceptions may enable a 16-year-old the right to sign certain contracts.

136. (3) Continuous, open, and notorious use must be established for 15 years to acquire an easement by prescription.

137. (3) An easement may be extinguished if the owner of the dominant estate gains open and continuous control and possession of the property for the prescriptive period of 15 years.

138. (1) When the owner of a property seeks to prevent another's acquisition of an easement, he or she must abide by statutory procedures. Posting of "No Trespassing" signs, letters, and/or verbal contact with the person claiming the right will not qualify as an interruption in most cases.

139. (3) Continuous use, hostile to the owner, must be established for at least 15 years to acquire title by adverse possession.

140. (4) Adverse possession must be possession that is adverse to the owner, i.e. without the owner's consent or permission. Continuous, open (not private) use, hostile to the owner, must be established for 15 years to acquire title by adverse possession.

141. (3) A license is a temporary use of land that can be revoked. Apple picking one month a year is a temporary use, not a continuous possession.

142. (2) The new use is hostile and if not stopped, could become an easement by prescription if the statutory time frame of 15 years is met.

143. (4) Connecticut law requires that leases for more than one year be recorded in the local land record to give constructive notice to a third party in a manner similar to recording deeds. A notice of lease may be recorded in lieu of the lease itself.

144. (2) The provision is unenforceable, but the lease is still valid.

145. (4) The landlord should present the rules when the tenant is entering into the rental agreement or whenever the rules are adopted.

146. (2) If a tenant fails to pay rent within nine days from the due date, the landlord may terminate the lease and evict the tenant.

147. (2) Raising rents would not be deemed retaliatory and will be allowed when costs due to the tenant's lack of care of the property, property taxes, or other operating expenses have increased substantially at least four months before the landlord's request for the additional rent.

148. (4) The security deposit earns interest at a rate tied to the average savings deposit rate.

149. (2) The tenant must forfeit one month's interest for a late payment.

150. (2) The landlord may sue the tenant for the back rent.

151. (3) If an evicted tenant does not remove his or her belongings, the sheriff may place the belongings on the street.

152. (3) After 30 days, all proceeds are turned over to the town treasury. The landlord does not benefit from this sale.

153. (4) Within 30 days of the date that the lease ends, the landlord must return the security deposit (and applicable accrued interest) to the tenant. If there have been damages to the property by the tenant, the landlord is entitled to keep all or a portion of the security deposit, but must give the tenant an itemized list of the damages within the 30 days.

154. (1) In Connecticut, the law regarding security deposits applies to all residential landlords, regardless of the size of the complex. Within 30 days of the date that the lease ends, the landlord must return the security deposit (and applicable accrued interest) to the tenant. If, however, there have been damages to the property by the tenant, the landlord is entitled to keep all or a portion of the security deposit, but must give the tenant an itemized list of the damages within the 30 days.

155. (2) Leases for over one year need to be in writing to be enforceable. There is no requirement that this writing be on any type of standard form. Connecticut law requires that leases for more than one year (or a notice of lease) be recorded in the local land record to give constructive notice to a third party in a manner similar to recording deeds; nonrecording will not affect the enforceability between the parties.

156. (2) In all cases in Connecticut where a tenancy is not subject to an agreed upon term or expiration date, it is construed as a month-to-month tenancy. For a month-to-month tenancy, a landlord is required to give a tenant one month's notice to terminate.

157. (3) The landlord can require up to two months' rent as a security deposit, in this example, $1,500.

158. (1) The security deposit, with any interest owed, must be returned within 30 days. The landlord must explain any deductions withheld.

159. (3) In the event that a tenant abandons the property, the landlord is required to make a reasonable effort to re-rent the property to minimize the tenant's liability. If the landlord is able to re-rent, the landlord must deduct this amount from the amount of rent still owed by the tenant. Here, the original tenant owed three months' rent, but the landlord was able to recapture two months' rent so the liability of the original tenant would only be one month's rent.

160. (1) The tenant can be arrested. A tenant who intentionally damages leased property is considered to have committed a crime and can be criminally prosecuted. A tenant would only lose his or her security deposit up to the amount of monetary damages.

161. (1) State statute requires that deeds conveying title must be recorded within a reasonable time of delivery.

162. (4) In Connecticut, the town clerk is responsible for recording deeds and maintenance of the land records.

163. (2) Name changes must be recorded within 60 days.

164. (1) A homeowner's only right to redeem property being foreclosed through a strict foreclosure process in Connecticut is on the law day provided by the court.

165. (3) In Connecticut, a homeowner does not have an equitable or statutory right of redemption; i.e., to redeem the property before or after title passes to the foreclosing creditor or highest bidder. The only way that an owner may redeem property being foreclosed at a foreclosure sale is by being the successful bidder.

166. (4) In Connecticut, a homeowner does not have an equitable or statutory right of redemption; i.e., to redeem the property before or after title passes to the foreclosing creditor or highest bidder. The only way that an owner may redeem property being foreclosed at a foreclosure sale is by being the successful bidder.

167. (3) State statues require physical revaluation of real property every 12 years.

168. (3) Real estate is taxed at the municipal level in Connecticut. The amount of tax is based on the value of the property.

169. (2) Taxes are payable on July 1 and January 1. The tax year in Connecticut is generally the same as the state's fiscal year and runs from July 1 to June 30. In the majority of Connecticut towns, real property taxes are payable for the current year on July 1 and January 1 (six-month taxes on each date).

170. (3) In Connecticut, from a strictly legal standpoint, property taxes become a lien on the property from the date of assessment (generally October 1) but this lien is never enforced by law unless the taxpayer violates the prescribed payment schedule.

171. (1) The conveyance tax is based on the sale price.

172. (3) Environmentally impacted or contaminated sites may be eligible for tax abatement if remedied and redeveloped. They are assessed at market value (which may be essentially nil because of the desirability of such property). For tax purposes, farm, forest, and open space land are not assessed at market value. If the owners of such land follow the proper registration procedures, their assessments are lowered to provide considerable tax relief.

173. (1) A property owner may appeal the assessment to the local board of tax review.

174. (3) Connecticut does not require that a deed state the actual consideration paid for a property. Since the amount of town conveyance tax is always stamped on a recorded deed, the purchase price can be calculated. This is done by dividing the town conveyance tax paid by the conveyance tax rate, which is currently .0011. $192.50 divided by .0011= $175,000.

175. (2) There is no conveyance tax on a transfer of property pursuant to a condemnation proceeding.

176. (4) The municipal conveyance tax rate is .0011, so the municipal conveyance tax is .0011 x $250,000 = $275. The state conveyance tax rate is .005, so the state conveyance tax is .005 x $250,000 = $1,250. Added together, the total conveyance tax is $1,525.

177. (3) The municipal conveyance tax rate is .0011, so the municipal conveyance tax is .0011 x $185,000 = $203.50.

178. (1) The municipal conveyance tax rate is .0011, so the municipal conveyance tax is .0011 x $150,000 = $165. The state conveyance tax rate is .005, so the state conveyance tax is .005 x $150,000 = $750. Added together, the total conveyance tax is $915. The mortgage amount is immaterial.

179. (2) A person aggrieved by a real estate licensee may recover a maximum compensation of $25,000. The aggrieved person must first sue and obtain a final judgment against the licensee, and then show that he/she was unable to collect that judgment.

180. (2) The guaranty fund's purpose is to provide a means of compensation for actual monetary losses suffered by individuals as a result of the acts of a licensee who has violated the license law or committed other illegal acts related to a real estate transaction.

181. (2) Connecticut law itemizes who may receive compensation from the fund. One example is a payment to a seller who pays a commission to a broker under false pretenses. These funds are not available to a buyer who pays a fee to a broker under a buyer agency agreement, nor to brokers who do not receive their commissions.

182. (3) A person aggrieved by a real estate licensee may recover a maximum compensation of $25,000 from the real estate guaranty fund.

183. (2) When the commission makes a payment from the fund to satisfy a claim, the license of the broker or salesperson whose actions were the cause of the claim will automatically be revoked (not just suspended). The license will not be reissued until the person has repaid the entire sum plus interest.

184. (2) Connecticut law specifically states that the level of the fund shall not exceed $500,000.

185. (3) When the commission makes a payment from the fund to satisfy a claim, the license of the broker or salesperson whose actions were the cause of the claim will automatically be revoked (not just suspended). The license will not be reissued until the person has repaid the entire sum plus interest.

186. (2) Any action that might involve subsequent recovery from the guaranty fund must be initiated within two years from the date of the final judgment or on expiration of time for an appeal. In this example, the client must file a claim by December 20, 2001.

187. (4) Connecticut does not recognize either dower or curtesy. The interest of a person in the property of his or her spouse is provided for via statutory survivorship rights.

188. (1) Under Connecticut statutes relating to the property rights of a surviving spouse, the husband will be entitled to a life estate equal in value to one-third of the deceased partner's property, both real and personal.

189. (1) Connecticut does not recognize either dower or curtesy. Under Connecticut statutes relating to the property rights of a surviving spouse, the husband would be entitled to a life estate equal in value to one-third of the deceased partner's property, both real and personal.

190. (4) Connecticut law does not recognize tenancy by the entirety.

191. (1) When a husband and wife hold real estate as joint tenants and subsequently obtain a divorce, the divorce decree usually serves to extinguish the joint tenancy and converts it into a tenancy in common.

192. (3) A marketable record title is one that is unbroken for a period of 40 years.

193. (3) Any conveyance to a husband and wife in Connecticut, without specific language indicating otherwise, would be treated in the same manner as a conveyance to two or more unrelated parties as a tenancy in common.

194. (2) Title passes upon delivery and acceptance of a deed, in this example, November 15.

195. (2) In Connecticut, it is not necessary for a non-owning spouse to sign any conveyance of an owning spouse's real estate since there are no statutory survivorship rights that attach to property while the owning spouse is alive. There is never a need for a tenant to sign a listing agreement.

196. (3) If a person has lost or misplaced his or her original deed, a copy of this deed from the public records will serve as prima facie evidence of the title.

197. (3) Each of the 169 towns in Connecticut maintains land records where documents affecting title to property within the town are recorded.

198. (1) The town clerk maintains lists separate from all other recorded documents containing information on local real estate transactions indexed under the names of the grantors and grantees. The grantor list shows transactions indexed under grantors.

199. (1) In Connecticut, if a property is navigable, upland property owners' boundaries extend to the water's edge, which is the mean high tide line.

200. (3) A riparian landowner cannot unreasonably contain, divert, or destroy the nonnavigable stream, but may use water while it runs over his land.

201. (1) The Connecticut Real Estate Commission is authorized to write rules and regulations that have the force of law. Exam questions are written by an independent testing service and reviewed by the real estate commission. The testing service administers the exams. The legislature enacts law.

202. (3) Each town sets its own tax rate, which is referred to as the mill rate.